An Introduction and Translation of

Gli Experimenti de la Excellentissima Signora Caterina da Forlì

(The Experiments of Caterina Sforza of Forli)

GIGI COULSON

Copyright © 2016 Gigi Coulson

All rights reserved.

ISBN: 153523816X
ISBN-13: 978-1535238168

DEDICATION

For Coey, the love of my life.
For Geri, who loved me even before I was born.
For Barbara, who showed me how to love Jehovah.
For Gary, Tyriee and Taylor, who I love dearly.

ABOUT THE AUTHOR

Gigi Coulson lives in New Orleans and, in her real life, is a biologist, sociologist, and ethnographer. She has a graduate degree in the sociology of natural resource management. Her 15-year career in environmental planning has given her a chance to effect changes in the way social impacts are assessed along with environmental impacts while NEPA is being followed. Aside from the fulfillment of her work life, Gigi loves to study history and volunteers with an international non-profit educational organization to reach others about life in Medieval and Renaissance Italy. Her historical research is focused on the 14th and 15th centuries in norther Italy. Her main interests are women's lives, sociocultural development, herbalism, fashion, and alchemy. She travels to Venice, Ferrara, and Bologna often to conduct research for her classes and publications.

Laureata in la sociologia, la silvicoltura, e scienze ambientali, la mia grande passione è la rievocazione storica medievale e rinascimento. Il periodo di cui mi occupo è la seconda metà del XIV secolo e il cinquecento en Ferrara, Venezia, e Firenze. Mi interessano in particolare la cultura materiale, la storia della moda, soprattutto quella femminile, e la storia della alchimia. Amo sia il lavoro di ricerca su fonti iconografiche e documentarie sia cimentarmi in tentativi ricostruttivi, in particolare legati all'ambito erboristeria.

You can visit her blog at https://labelladonna.net/

Table of Contents

Introduction 6
Gli Experimenti 7
Measurements 10
The Recipes 11
   Hair 11
   Skin 13
   Teeth and Mouth 20
   Life (Immortality) 22
Conclusion 23
Glossary 24
Bibliography 27
Appendix A – Gli Experimenti Recipes (from Passolini Volume III, 1893) 29

The purpose of this booklet is to provide a brief introduction to an important collection of recipes as well as translations of 24 of the recipes for living history participants interested in still room arts as practiced during the Italian Renaissance (1400-1600). To my knowledge these recipes are not available in English, so I took on this project to add a new resource to the catalog of information available.

Introduction

Today we buy beauty products and medicine made by cosmetic and pharmaceutical companies in shops, drugstores, and department stores. During the Renaissance beauty products and herbal medicines were made in the workshops of monasteries, still rooms of homes large and small, or by alchemists in their storefronts (Eamon 1996). These arts were part of traditions handed down from Arab, Roman, Greek, and Turkish cultures (Eamon 1996). Every family had its own book of secrets (*Libretti di Secreti, Tesori, Tesoretti*) where they recorded successful iterations of their personal recipes for cosmetics, medicines, and household products such as dyes, candles, pesticides, etc.(Eamon 1996). One example of this type of book is Caterina Sforza's alchemical, medical experiment, and recipe collection titled *Gli Experimenti de la Ex.ma S.r Caterina da Furlj Matre de lo inllux.mo S.r Giouanni de Medici*[1], or *Gli Experimenti*[2].

After her death the *ricettario*[3] were passed down to her son, Giovanni dalle Bande Nere (Passolini vI 1893). The manuscript contained 454 recipes divided into 358 medicinal, 30 chemical, and 66 cosmetic categories and handwritten in Italian vernacular sprinkled with Latin (Catellani 2014). The recipes were transcribed from her manuscript in 1525 by a captain in Giovanni's army, Count Lucantonio Cuppano da Montefalco (Passolini vI 1893). The transcription was then handed down to Giovanni's son Grand Duke Cosimo I de' Medici, then Grand Duke Francesco I, and finally to Don Antonio de' Medici. Don Antonio was the benefactor of Antonio Neri, a famous 17th Century *conciatore*[4] in Florence who also used Caterina's recipes (Lev 2011). Antonio Neri is remembered mostly for his book on glassmaking, *L'Arte Vetraria*. Caterina's recipes were ultimately published as a book by Pier Passolini in 1893. Included in *Gli Experimenti* are an assortment of formulas which range from cosmetics, to medical remedies, poisons and alchemical concoctions (Passolini vIII 1893).

---

[1] Gli experimenti de la excellentissima signora Caterina da Forlì Matre de lo inlluxtrissimo signor Giovanni de Medici (Experiments of the Most Excellent Lady Caterina from Forli mother of the Most Illustrious Lord Giovanni of the Medici)

[2] The Experiments, plural

[3] Recipes, plural

[4] A specialist in alchemy who formulated glass from raw materials

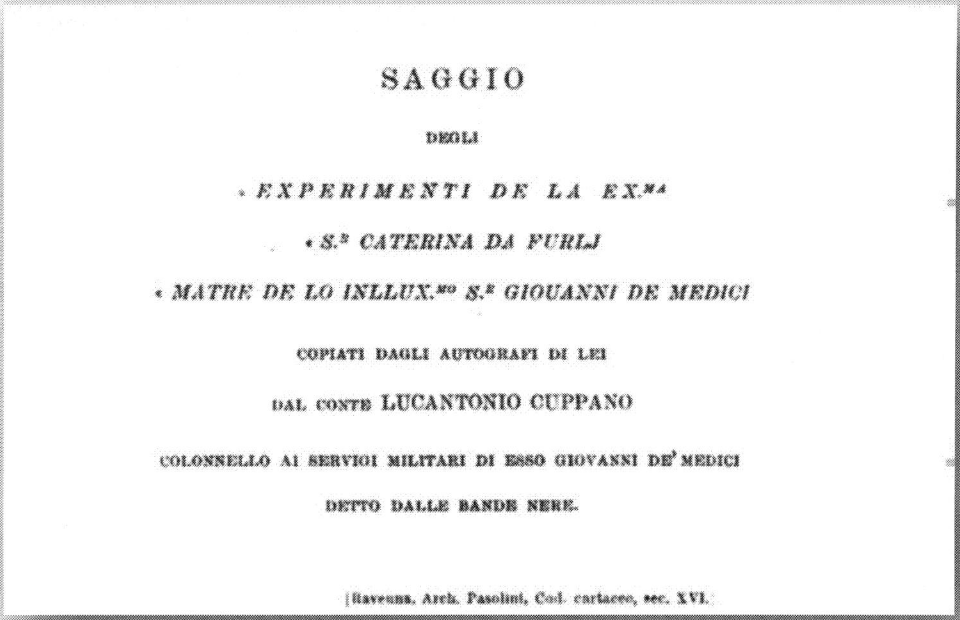
SAGGIO

DEGLI

« EXPERIMENTI DE LA EX.MA

« S.A CATERINA DA FURLJ

« MATRE DE LO INLLUX.MO S.R GIOUANNI DE MEDICI

COPIATI DAGLI AUTOGRAFI DI LEI

DAL CONTE LUCANTONIO CUPPANO

COLONNELLO AI SERVIGI MILITARI DI ESSO GIOVANNI DE' MEDICI

DETTO DALLE BANDE NERE.

(Ravenna, Arch. Pasolini, Cod. cartaceo, sec. XVI.)

Figure 1 Title Page of Volume III (Passolini 1893, p600)

Caterina was the Countess of Imola and Forli who ruled fairly but firmly and commanded her own armies, carrying on the Sforza family tradition of "strength" as her forefathers came to power in Milan as mercenary soldiers (Lev 2011). *Gli Experimenti* is an extensive catalog of recipes and would have taken several years to develop (Passolini vIII 1893). Many of the recipes had *è provato*[5] noted next to them in the margins of the manuscript page (Passolini vIII 1893). Despite all of the political turmoil in the Italian City-States Caterina still took the time to sharpen her mind, care for herself, and care for her family by refining her "experiments". Her curiosity for the alchemical sciences spurred her to perform endless iterations, which she based on the input of Ludovico Albertini, an herbalist from Forlì who shared his knowledge and works of alchemy with Caterina (Passolini vI 1893). She also devoted herself to correspondence with doctors, pharmacists, noblewomen, and sorcerers who could advise her on refining her remedies (Passolini vIII 1893).

Gli Experimenti

The document is valuable for many reasons, one is because it gives us insight into the state of scientific knowledge at the end of the 15th Century. The era was certainly full of superstitions but it also used the principle of modern homeopathy *similia similibu curantur*[6] (Rovesti 1975). For example, the root of the celandine (which means swallow) produces caustic milk that removes hair, so alchemists also have a recipe for distilled swallows to do the same (Caruso 2009). Similarly, Caruso (2009) explains that alchemists used fennel (*finocchio*) to improve vision (*occhio fino*). Another reason this document is so valuable is that it may be the most complete document we have on medicine and cosmetic arts of the 15th Century (Rovesti 1975).

---

[5] Meaning tried or proven (Florio 1611)

[6] Like cures like

The largest group of her recipes is medicinal in nature, require long preparation times, and involve complicated methods. There are cures for diseases, aids for sleep, concoctions to promote fertility, abortifacents, healing balms, teas to cure melancholy, male impotence fixes, honeymoon pleasure enhancers, antispasmotics[7], digestive aids[8], and anesthetics for surgery (Caruso 2009). Caterina's anesthetic is remarkable in that its ingredients are (besides being dangerous analgesics) the same as used by the famous *Scuola Medica Salernitana*[9], recorded in a 13th Century surgery handbook published in Bologna (Salvadori 2003). The anesthetic is comprised of opium, unripe blackberry juice, mandrake leaves, ivy, and hemlock, among other plants. Caterina writes that this recipe is (Catellani 2014):

> *"To make a person sleep in such fashion that you will be able to operate in surgery anything you wish and he will not feel you and it is proven"*

Many of the recipes are focused on enhancing and preserving beauty. They are divided into cosmetics, lotions, creams, elixirs, liquids, and ointments[10]. These were very dear to Caterina, as she was known for her beauty and likely wanted to remain so as she aged (Lev 2011). Many of the beauty problems and medical problems of 15th Century women are the same ones we deal with today. Caterina developed formulations to darken the skin, lose weight, lift up sagging flesh, and to make the hair curly. Others were used to make the hands white, clear the skin of blemishes, grow hair, dye hair, remove hair, provide red color for the cheeks, and scent the breath.

---

[7] Contra spasimo (Passolini v.III page 687)

[8] Olio che conforta lo stomach el core et Le Rene (Passolini v.III page 685)

[9] Medical School of Salerno

[10] Cosmetici, lozioni, crème, elisir, lisci, and pomate (Passolini v. III)

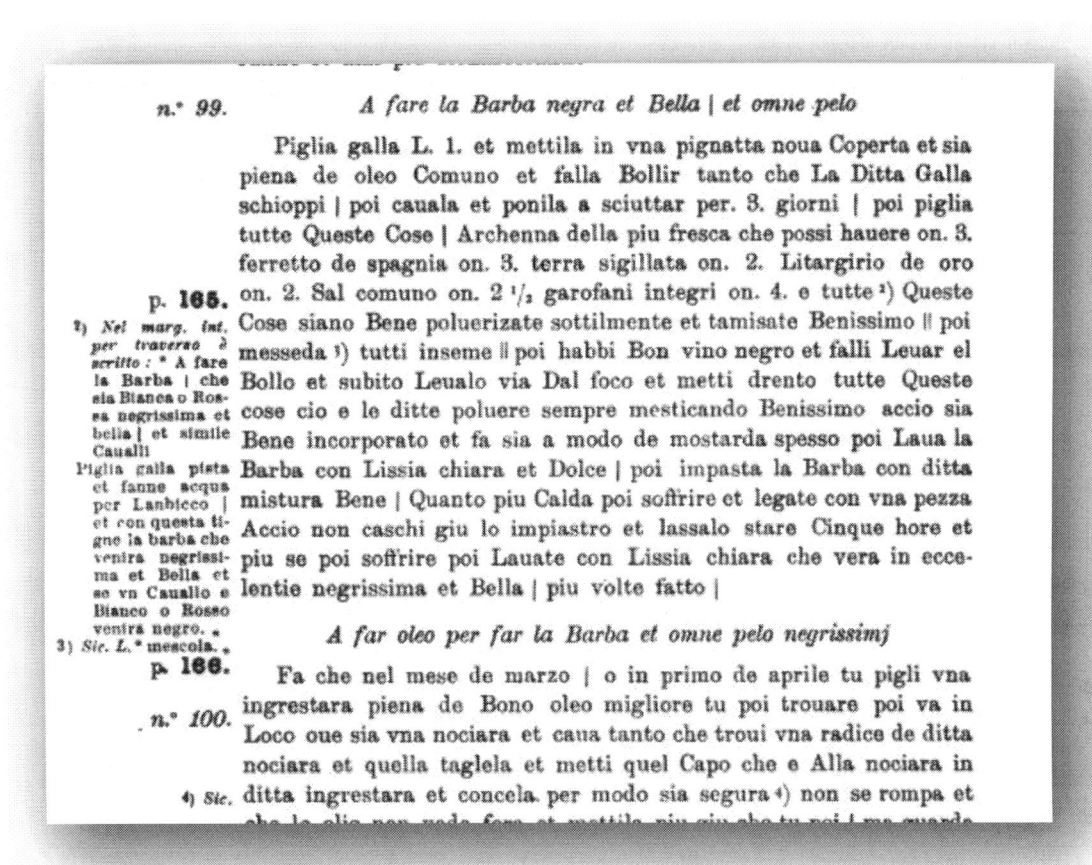

Figure 2 Recipes # 99 and #100 showing how Caterina's marginal notes are recorded (Passolini 1893, p660, Original Cuppano p165-6)

Caterina suggests dust of baked frogs, lizards, and bees to regrow hair; promotes vegetable mastic to remove hair; and developed a recipe for *de Levante*[11] with a brazilwood[12] base to redden the cheeks (mixing rock alum, lime, and brazilwood). She recommends removing the lime when the skin reddens. Her skin whitening recipes include *cerussa* (white lead) which was known to be harmful to ingest but thought to be ok to apply to the skin (Caruso 2009). The most famous recipe is *L'Acqua Celeste*[13], which she writes is "of such virtue that makes the old young again… the dead alive… and the sick well… within the space of 3 pater nosters". The water was a tonic of sorts containing distilled waters of sage, basil, rosemary, clove, mint, nutmeg, elderberry, red rosewater, white rosewater, and anise (Catellani 2014). Alchemists were very concerned with developing potions capable of imparting immortality and many "miraculous waters" were developed in the late 14th Century, including the famous Queen of Hungary Water (Eamon 1994).

---

[11] Literally, "wake up"

[12] Caesalpinia echinata, also known as pernambuco

[13] Celestial Water

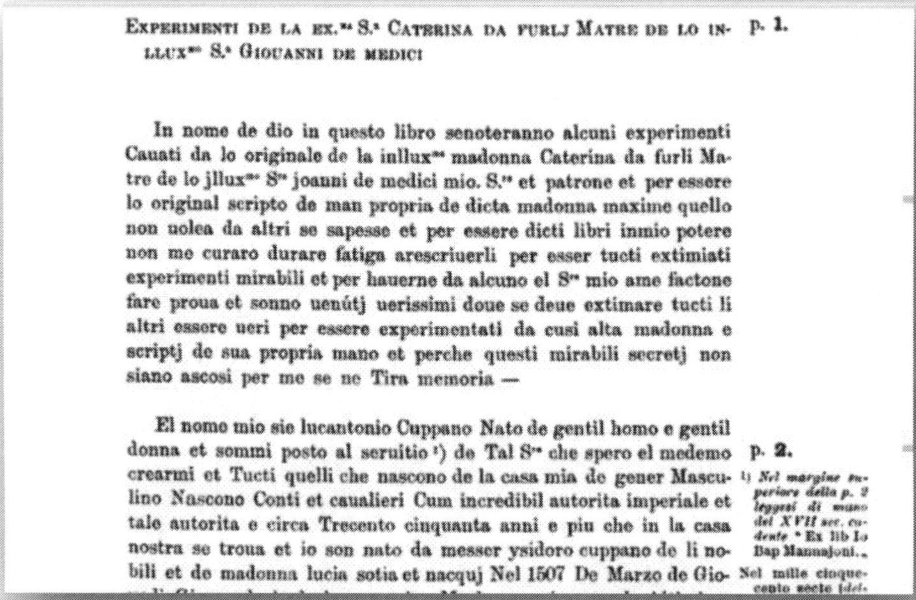

Figure 3 Introduction to Gli Experimenti (Passolini 1893 p617)

Measurements

Before I list the recipes let me make a few statements about the measurement system used in the 15th Century. There was no standard for measurement on the Italian peninsula until the 19th Century (Zupko 1981). The measurements used in *Gli Experimenti* would have had different values depending in which City-State it was taken. For my translations I used measurement reference information from Ferrara (a central area in the middle of the territories of Venice, Milan, Florence, and Bologna) from a book titled *Italian Weights and Measures from the Middle Ages to the Nineteenth Century* (Zupko 1981).

Unit Name	English Name	Grams	Relationship
Scrupolo	*Scruple*	*1.198 grams*	-
Dramma	*Dragme*	*3.595 grams*	*3 scrupolo*
Oncia, Onza	*Ounce*	*27.25 grams*	*8 dramma*
Sodella, Scudella	-	*237 grams*	-
Libra, Libbra, Livra	*Pound*	*328 grams*	*12 oncia*
Anfora	*Amphora*	*2 Liters*	-
Quarta, Quarto	*Quart*	*0.089 Liters*	-

*Source: Zupko 1981, Ferrarese Units of Measure

Marriott et al (2006) noted that "ij" and "iij" denote units, where two or more units are expressed together with the final unit expressed as "j". Half is expressed by "ss" or "fs" (Marriott 2006).

The Recipes

Hair

Per far crescere li Capelli (To make the hair grow)

Si prepara un semplice decotto con una manciata di malva, del trifoglio, del prezzemolo e con questo decotto si fanno diversi lavaggi (Caruso 2009).

Prepare a simple decoction with a handful of mallow, clover, and parsley and with this decoction wash the hair many times.

A far li capelli biondi come oro (To make the hair blonde like gold)

Piglia radiche de ellera et radile bene et tritale menute et cavane acqua per lambicco et con ditta acqua bagnia el capo con una spognia et in otto giorni veniranno come oro (Passolini v.III p658)

Take the roots of the ivy plant and skin them and mince them and squeeze water out of them, distill this water and use a sponge to rinse the head with it and in eight days the hair will shine like gold.

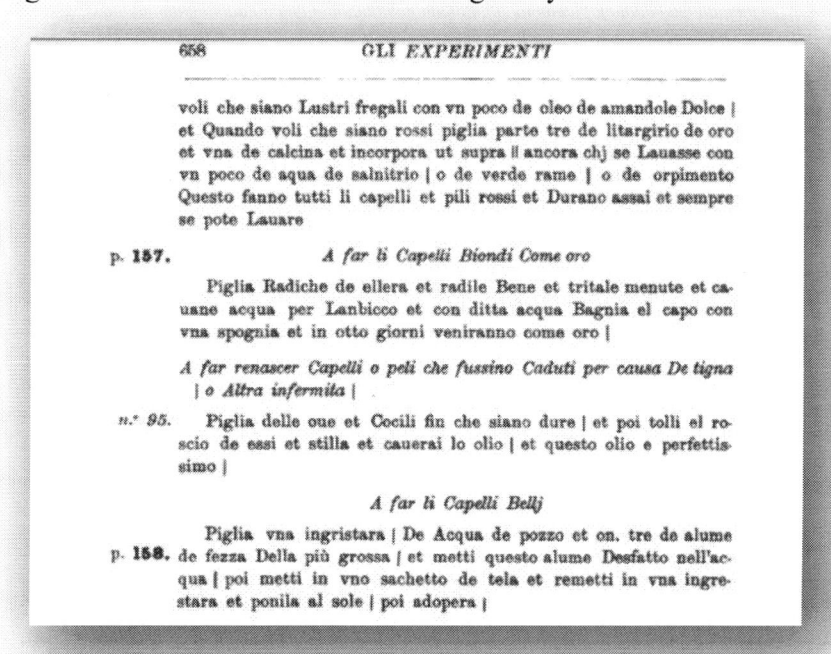

Figure 4 To Make the Hair Blonde Like Gold (Passolini 1893, p658)

A far Capelli biondi et come oro (To make the hair blond and like gold)

Piglia cinabro zaffrano et solfo et fa destillare queste cose per lanbicco et quando te hai lavato el capo, pettinate al sole et bagnia el pettine spesso in questa acqua stillata et cusi te asciutta al sole, et verra bella come oro (Passolini v.III p 657)

Take cinnabar, saffron, and sulfur and distill in an alembic[14], and when you have washed your hair, comb it in the sun, rinsing the comb often in this distilled water and then dry your hair in the sun and it will be beautiful like gold.

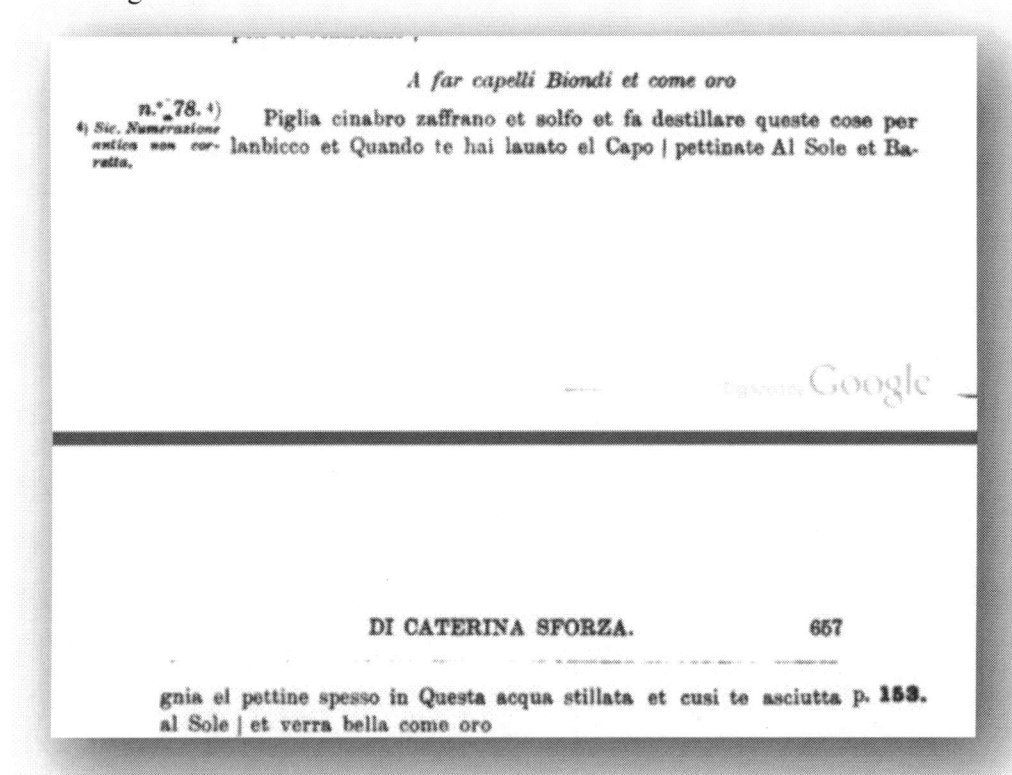

Figure 5 To Make the Hair Blonde and Like Gold (Passolini 1893, p657)

Per far li capelli biondi che durano doi mesi (To make the hair blonde so it will last two months)

Far bollire delle foglie di ellera et falle bollir in lissia cio e in quella che tu fai in casa et che bolla bene et con qualla lavati el capo et farai li capelli belli et volento far meglio piglia del Legnio de hellera et brusalo et fanne cenere et con quella cenere et ditte foglie fa la tua lissia et adopera (Passolini v. III p 653).

Boil the leaves of ivy along with your household lye and after it bubbles wash your head with it and have beautiful hair, and if wanting to make it better make the lye with ashes of the stems and leaves of the ivy, which makes your lye a better endeavor[15].

A far capelli biondi et belli per unaltro modo (To make the hair blonde)

Piglia semenza di ortiga et falla bollir in la lissia che fai con la tua cenere. Al solito et lavate et veneranno bellissimi (Passolini v. III p 653).

---

[14] An alembic is an apparatus used in distillation

[15] To make the recipe even more effective Caterina recommended putting three pieces of rhubarb root into the decoction to infuse for an entire day. After wet a linen cloth with it, wrap the hair, leave it on until almost dry and the hair will "undoubtedly shine like gold."

Piglia semenza de ortiga et falla bollire in la lissa cime fai con la tua cenere et lava et bellissimi (Catellani 2014).

Take nettle seeds and boíl them along with ashes to make lye. Wash your hair with this as usual and have beautiful hair.

A far cadere peli che mai più torneranno (To make hair drop out and never come back)

Piglia polvere de botte, farina de lupini, alume de rocco arso an on ij et falle bollire con uno boccale de acqua et, come leva el bollire, tolli dal fuoco et colale per feltro et lassa reposare nel vaso per otto giorni poi laa el loco dove voli che vada vial j peli con acqua poi bagnia; poi bagna una spugna in detta acqua et bagna il loco dove voli pelar più volte e tutti li peli cascheranno e mai piu renasceranno (Passolini v.III p660).

Take powder of *botte*[16], lupin bean flour, 2 ounces burnt rock alum[17], and boil them with one jug of water and when it bubbles remove from the fire and filter it and let it rest in the pot for eight days; then wet a sponge in this water and wet the spot where you don't want hair several times and all the hair will fall out and not grow back.

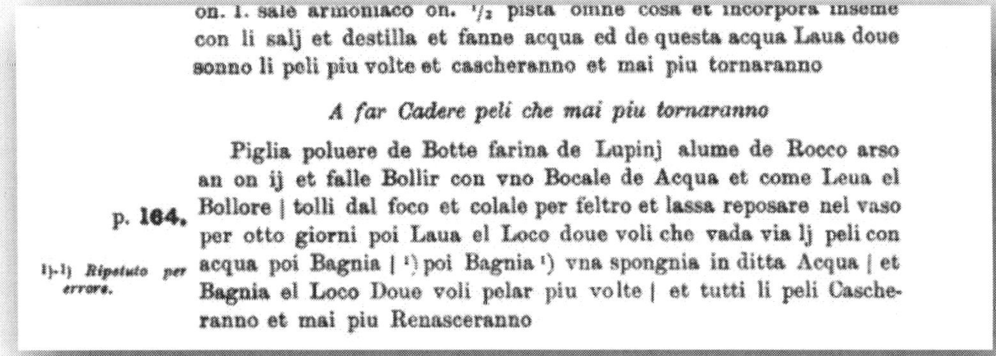
on. I. sale armoniaco on. 1/2 pista omne cosa et incorpora inseme con li salj et destilla et fanne acqua ed de questa acqua Laua doue sonno li peli piu volte et cascheranno et mai piu tornaranno

A far Cadere peli che mai piu tornaranno

Piglia poluere de Botte farina de Lupinj alume de Rocco arso an on ij et falle Bollir con vno Bocale de Acqua et come Leua el Bollore | tolli dal foco et colale per feltro et lassa reposare nel vaso per otto giorni poi Laua el Loco doue voli che vada via lj peli con acqua poi Bagnia | [1]) poi Bagnia [1]) vna spongnia in ditta Acqua | et Bagnia el Loco Doue voli pelar piu volte | et tutti li peli Cascheranno et mai piu Renasceranno

p. **164.**

1)-1) *Ripetuto per errore.*

Figure 6 To Make the Hair Drop Out (Passolini 1893, p660)

Skin

Per far la faccia bianchissima et bella et colorita (To make the face white, beautiful, and colorful)

Mescolare dello zucchero con del bianco d'uovo[18] e acqua di bryonia (Bryonia dioica). Con questo miscuglio ci si deve bagnare il viso (Caruso 2009).

Mix sugar with egg whites and red byrony water. With this mixture you should wash your face.

Aqua per fare la faccia bianchissima et bella et lucente et colorita (Water to make the face white, beautiful, shining, and colorful)

---

[16] I could not find a translation of this word

[17] Rock Alum is a double sulphate of aluminum and potassium, formerly used to fix dye colors and fabrics and to manufacture cosmetics

[18] This could be the literal white of the egg or egg tempera

Piglia chiara de ova fresca quante tu voli et falli destillare a lanbicco et con quella aqua lava la faccia, che e perfettissima a far bello et leva tutti li segni et cicatrice della faccia (Passolini v.III p627).

Piglia chiara de ove et falla distillar in alambicco et con quella aqua lava la faccia che e perfectissima a far bella et leva tutti li segni et cicatrici (Catellani 2014).

Take egg whites and distill in an alembic and with this water wash your face which is most perfect to make it beautiful and remove all marks or scars.

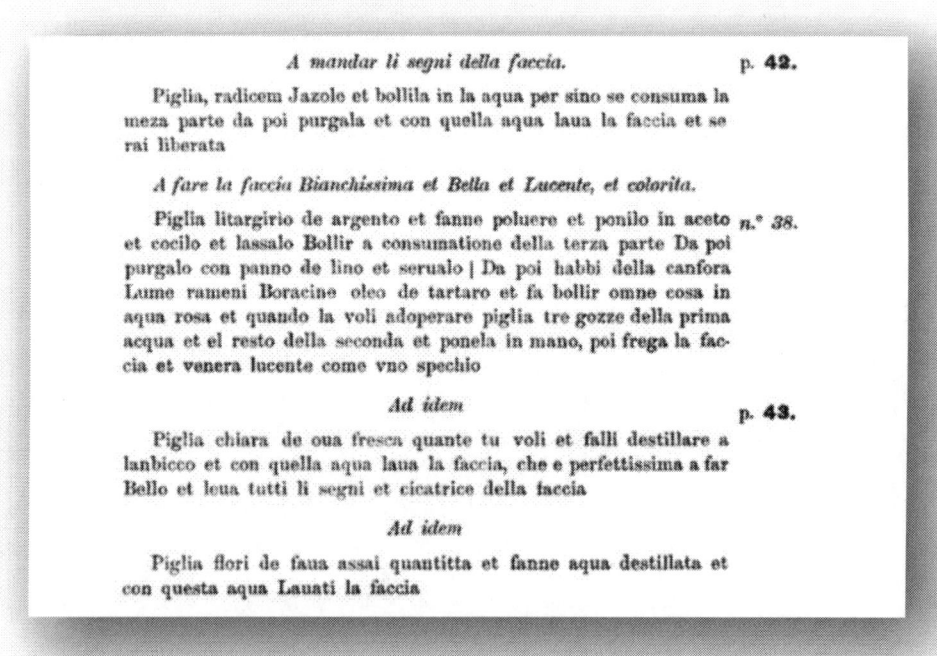

Figure 7 To Make the Face White (Passolini 1893, p627)

Contro la rosseza de viso per causa sole et crepature (Against redness of the face caused by the sun and cracking)

Piglia cerusa aqua rosa oleo de viole et mestica inseme et ugne la faccia (Passolini v.III p630).

Piglia cerusica et aqua de rosa et oleo violato ed incorpora insieme et mestica bene poin ogniti la faccia et e perfectissimma (Catellani 2014).

Take white lead and rosewater and oil of violets and incorporate together and blend them well then anoint the face with this and it will be most perfect.

> 630　　　　　　　GLI EXPERIMENTI
>
> p. 50.　　　　　　　ad idem
>
> Piglia vitriolo Romano on iiij salnitrio on iij limatura achi | on. 1, et destilla alanbicco et piglia della prima aqua on ½ et ponili in essa 3 on de canfora et con questa fregate la faccia
>
> a guarire la Roseza del volto
>
> n.° 39.　Piglia Cerusa aqua rosa oleo de viole et mestica inseme et ugne la faccia
>
> Ad idem
>
> Piglia Solforo viuo on. 1. incenso Bianco on ij mirra on | ij | canfora on | ij | et de tutte queste cose fa poluere et mistica con libra vna de aqua rosa et la sera quando vai adormire piglia vn poco de questa aqua et ognete la faccia et la matina lauate con aqua de fonte |

Figure 8 To Cure Redness of the Face (Passolini 1893, p630)

L'abbronzatura della pelle (To bronze the skin)

Piglia radice di mira el sole et radial et metila in bono vino che fara bonissimo colore et bello (Catellani 2014).

Take root of the 'flower of sun'[19] and grate it and put it in a good wine which will make the most good and beautiful color.

A far bella (To make beautiful)

Piglia aqua de pozo L una, salnitrio quarta ½, canfora ottava, sale comune on j, mistica inseme omne cosa et fa bollir da poi usala (Passolini v.III p629).

Take one pound well water, ½ quart saltpeter[20], 1/8 quart camphor, and 1 ounce common salt, mix all this together and boil them the usual way.

---

[19] Sunflower or girasole

[20] Potassium nitrate

> *a far bella*
>
> Piglia la radice della Bertonica et falla cocere in oleo et con questo lauate la faccia
>
> *A far Bella la faccia et leuar via omne lentigine et cicatrice et macchia* p. 48.
>
> Piglia litargirio de oro on |6| aceto vino bianco libra vna et meza | pista bene el litargirio et ponilo inseme con le sopraditte cose et fa bollir per sinche consumi la meta et con questo fregate la faccia
>
> *a far bella*
>
> Piglia aqua de pozzo L. vna . Salnitrio quarta ¹/₂ Canfora ottaua ¹/₂ Sale comune on. j . mistica inseme omne cosa et fa bollir Da poi vsala
>
> *a far bella et leuar le lentigine*
>
> Piglia del piretro quanto ne poi tener in mano et fallo bollir con aceto et con esso lauate la faccia.
>
> *ad idem*
>
> Piglia, galbano, aceto, vitrum melle et mistica omne cosa inseme et fallo a modo unguento, et quando vai a dormire ognete la faccia et la matina lauate con acqua chiara. p. 49.

Figure 9 To Make Beautiful (Passolini 1893, p629)

A far bella (To make beautiful)

Piglia sale comune L.1, biacca L.1/2, argento (salivato?) solimato on.1, canfora on.1, argento vivo on.1 – ogne cosa fa bollire in uno bocale de acqua che si consumi el terzio, dapoi, adopera et lavate le mano et el viso quando voli (Passolini v.III p 634).

Take 1 pound common salt, ½ pound white lead, 1 ounce silver sage, 1 ounce camphor, and 1 ounce quicksilver. Boil everything in a bottle of water until reduced by a third, then wash your hands and face with this as you will.

> rali Dolce con la aqua de frasanella et De giglio
>
> *A far Bella*
>
> Piglia Sale comuno L. 1. Biaccha L. ½ argento solimato on. 1. canfora on. 1. argento viuo on. 1. ogne cosa fa bollire in vno bocale de aqua che si consumi el terzo dapoi adopera et lauate le mano et el viso quando volj
>
> *A far Bella*
>
> Piglia litargirio de oro spoluerizato on. ij. aceto forte bianco on ij cocilo tanto remanga on. ij. et e fatto et adopera
>
> *A far Bella*
>
> p. 69. Piglia aqua rosata o uero canfora on ij alume de piuma on ij Sale comuno on. j. et metti a bullire in ditta aqua et bulli et poi metti a freddare et de poi mestiga con muschio o altro come a te piace | la operatione de queste doi aque sono queste Tolli nella pianta della mano tanto de luna quanto delaltra et con el dito mestica bene inseme et deuinera bianco a modo Latte et poi ognite el uiso et le mano quando vai adormire et cusi fa ogne sera quanto ate pare et non temer aque ne altra cosa et poi lauarti el viso come te pare. et vederai questa Cosa mirabile et nobilissima

Figure 10 To Make Beautiful (Passolini 1893, p634)

Acqua a far bella (Water to make beautiful)

Piglia aceto forte, limoni tagliati in pezzi et ponilo alambicco de vetrio et ponili de garofani fatti in polvere et garofani integri, poco de uno e delaltro, et metti ogni cosa alambicco, et salva l'acqua che è perfetta, et adopera (Passolini v.III p636)

Distill strong vinegar and sliced lemons and put this water into a glass alembic along with powdered cloves and whole cloves, a little of one and the other, and save this perfect water and use.

Aqua a far Bella

Piglia aceto forte | Limoni tagliati in pezzi et ponilo alanbicco de vetrio et ponili de garofani fatti in polvere et garofani integri n.° 46.

636 GLI EXPERIMENTI

poco de vno et delaltro | et metti ogni cosa alanbicco | et salua la aqua che e perfetta | et adopera

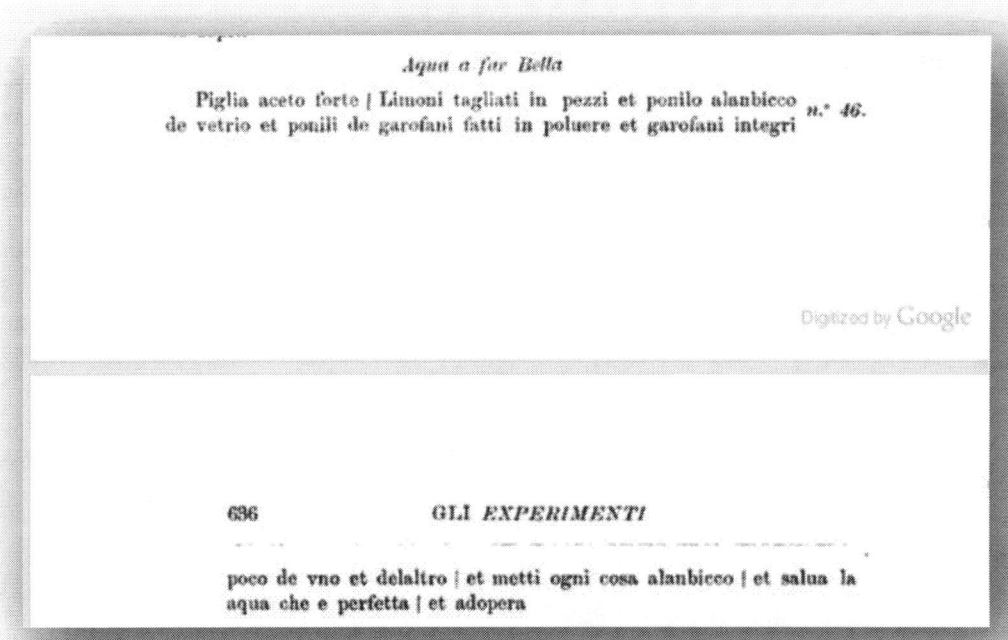

Figure 11 Water to Make Beautiful (Passolini 1893, p636)

Per far le mani bianche et belle tanto che pareranno de avorio (To make the hands white and beautiful like ivory)

Dai a lungo bollire ad acqua e crusca di grano finchè la mescolanza un poco si addensi. Poscia fai colar l'acqua e ancora calda metti in essa un pomo tagliato in tocchi e quando essa acqua sarà fredda lavatene le mani che resteranno bianche e morbide ed belle vedersi (Caruso 2009).

Boil water and wheat bran for a long time until the mixture thickens. Filter this water and reheat, put a sliced apple in it and when the water is cold wash the hands with this and they will remain soft, white, and beautiful.

A fare la mano et il viso bianco

Piglia foglie e radice de urtica e fa bulire in acqua et cum quel acqua lávate le mano e il volto e diventeranno bianche e morbide (Passolini v.III p622).

Take the leaves and roots of nettles and boil them in water and with this water wash the hands and the face when you want them to be white and soft.

A fare le mammelle piccole et dure alle donne (To make the breasts small and firm)

Piglia zusvese, una scudella de succo, et dello aceto bianco più forte come puoi e componi lo succo con lo aceto, poi bagnia pezze di canovaccio in ditta acqua et poni sopra el petto et poni doi tazzette di vetiio sopra pezze che vadano sopra tecte. Lega con una fascia longa, più stretto che poi, et cusi farai piccole dure et el petto bello (Catellani 2014).

Take enough zusvese[21] to make a cup of juice, the strongest white vinegar you can, and mix the juice with the vinegar, then wet pieces of cloth with the water and apply across the chest above and below the

---

[21] I was not able to find a translation for this word

breasts. Put two little cups of glass over the teats. Wrap with a long, narrow band tightly around. This way you have small and firm and beautiful breasts, and while you do this the woman will be chaste.

Rossetto ligiadrissimo et ecellentissimo (Rouge very light and most excellent)

Piglia sciandoli rossi on. Una, acqua vita[22] on tre, et pista sottilmente li sciandoli, et lassali Bagniare in ditta asqua per spatio de doi ore, bene poi cola, et questa colatura serrala in una ampolla de vitreo che non respiri, et quando voli adoperare, mondifica la facia. Da poi mette el rossetto, et questo basta fare omni giorno una volta, perche questo Rossetto Basta tanto et in questo mezzo Quanto piu se lava, tanto de magio vivacita ligiandria et bellezza deviene, onde fácilmente se comprende De Quanto longo intervallo, la *pezzetta de levante* a questa cieda, concio sia che quella ognie volta che la faccia sia Bagniata, se deturpa et questa et per un giorno appena dura, et questo come dico non teme acqua per otto giorni integri, ansi se conserva con mirabil Belleza (Passolini v III p648).

Take 1 ounce red sandalwood, 3 ounces grappa, and grind the sandalwood finely and let it soak well in the grappa for two hours, then strain it; and seal the strained liquid in an airtight glass vial. When you want to use it, first cleanse the face, then put on the rouge. And you only need to do this once each day, because this rouge is sufficient like that, and through these means: the more you wash, the more you will gain a magical vivacity, gracefulness, and beauty, so that it will easily last for this interval. The 'cloth of awakening', was used for this effect, but it happened that every time the face was washed, it spoiled the effect, and it only lasted for a day. But with this one, as I said, you need not avoid water for eight days; in fact it will stay on the face with amazing beauty.

Figure 12 Rouge for the Face (Passolini 1893, p648)

---

[22] Distilled wine, which can be substituted with brandy, vodka, or grappa (Scullly 1995)

Teeth and Mouth

Per far li denti bianchi et lucenti (To make the teeth white and shiny)

Prendi dei grossi gambi di rosmarino e falli abbruciare sin che diventino cenere. Metti detta cenere in una piccola pignatta con qualche foglia di rosmarino acciocchè ne prenda l'odore. Con detta cenere sfrega spesso li denti con una pezza di lino (Caruso 2009).

Get big stalks of rosemary and burn them until they become ashes. Put the ashes in a small pot with a few sprigs of rosemary in order that it can take on the smell. Rub the teeth with a piece of linen dabbed with the ashes[23],[24].

A far li denti chiari lucenti et belli (To make the teeth clear, shiny, and beautiful)

Piglia del gambo del rosamarino et fanne carboni, et da questi fanne polvere setacciata et metti ditta polvere in una pezza de lino et sfrega spesso li denti (Passolini v.III p662)

Take whole stems of rosemary and char them and pulverize this into powder, sift, and put the powder on a piece of linen and rub the teeth often with this.

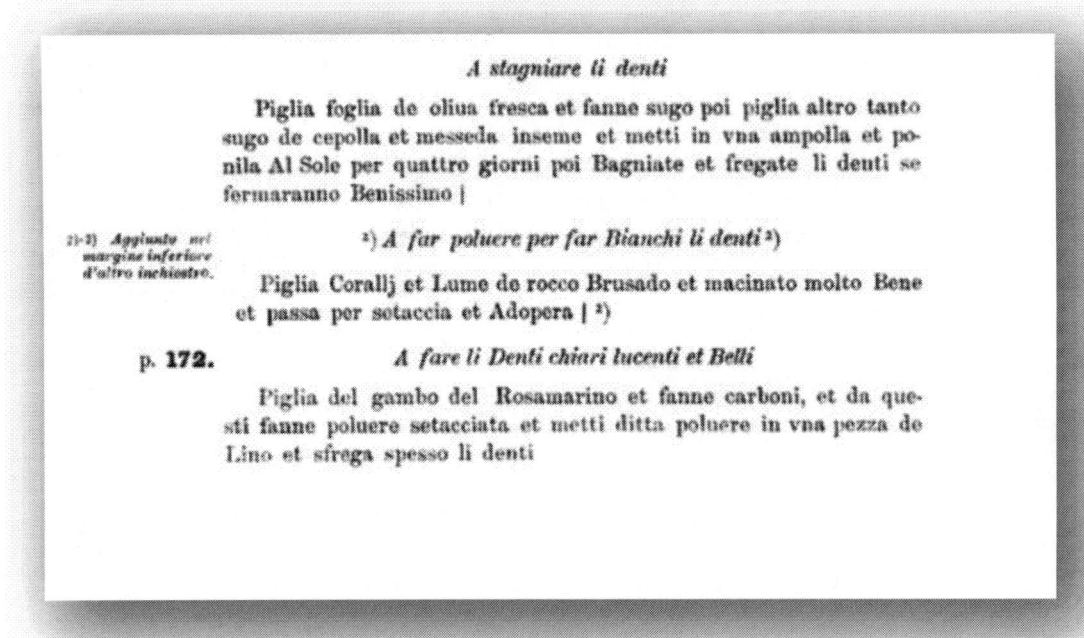

Figure 13 For the Teeth (Passolini 1893, p662)

Per avere un alito profumato (To have fragrant breath)

Piglia scorza di cetrangoli, noce moscata, chiodi di garofano, et cannella. Polverizzare il tutto ed impastarlo con del vino "et fanne pallottole et pigliane ante ed cibo et de poi el cibo" (Caruso 2009)

---

[23] Some of the teeth whitening recipes would horrify dentists today because they used abrasive powders which are highly damaging to the enamel. This recipe should be fine if used sporadically.

[24] To complete the effectiveness of the ashes of rosemary "after being rubbed with ashes wash the teeth and gums with some good wine".

Take citron peel, nutmeg, cloves, and cinnamon. Grind everything and mix with wine then "make little balls and chew before and after your meal[25]."

A fare odorare la bocca et el fiato (To make the pleasant the odor of the mouth and breath)

Piglia scorza de cedro, noce moscata, garofoni et salvia. Fa polvere, incorpora con vino et fanne pallattole et pigliane prima di el cibo et de poi del cibo (Catellani 2014).

Piglia scorza de cedro spigo, armatigo noce moscate garofani salu silio aloes pacanella mastica cubebe et de tutte queste cose fa polvere et incorpora con vino et fanne pallotte et pigliane nanti el cibo et de poi el cibo (Passolini v.III p 685).

Take cedar bark, nutmeg, cloves, and sage. Make a powder and incorporate wine and make little balls with it and chew them before and after your meal.

A guariré una persona a chi puzzasse la bocca o vero el fiato (To heal a person who has horrible breath)

Piglia 1 ounce garofani, 5 ounces cinamomo fino, 5 ounces tirats, con un terzo de finissimo vino fa pistare et fa bollire et danne mezzo bichieri per volta (Passolini v.III p 685).

Take 1 ounce cloves, 5 ounces ground cinnamon, 5 ounces tirats[26] (sic), and mix with a third of finest wine, then do grind and boil it and take a dose of half a glass at a time.

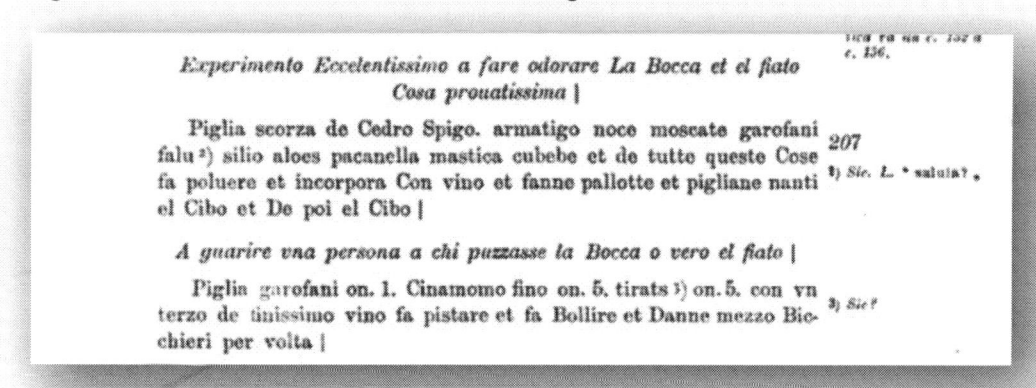

Figure 14 Two Mouth Freshening Recipes (Passolini 1893, p685)

A incarnar li denti (To enliven the teeth)

Piglia acqua de camomila on. 1, mele rosato colato on. Iij et mestica omne cosa inseme et bagnia delle pezze et poni su le gengive et muta spesso che se incarnaranno benissimo (Catellani 2014).

Take 1 ounce chamomile water, 3 ounces rose honey, and mix it all and dip some cloth pieces in it, and rub it on the gums, and change the cloth often so the gums will become firm and very well.

---

[25] The last lines after the recipe advise not to eat onion for a few days "and you shall see miracles."

[26] I could not find a translation for this word

Life (Immortality)

Aqua celeste che fa regiovanire la persona, et de morta fa vivo (Celestial water which makes a person younger and turns the dead into living)

Piglia garofani, noce moscate, zenzebero, benedi galenga pevero longo, pevero rotondo, grana de ginepro, scorza de cetrangoli, foglie de savia, foglie de basilico, de rosamarino, de maiorana fina, de menta totonda loribache pulegio gentiana calamento fior de sambuco rose bianche et roscie spigo nardo legno aloes culebe…(Passolini v.III p 639)

> Acqua Celeste se fa nel modo qui De sotto | et se po chiamar p. **87**.
> acqua De iouenezza et de vita cio e che fa regiouenire la persona
> et de morto fa viuo cio e si una persona fusse tanto grauata de in-
> fermitate che li medici labandonassino per incurabile et morta la
> reduce a sanita et se fa in questo modo
>
> Piglia garofani noce moscate zenzebero Benedi Galenga peuero
> Longo peuero rotondo grana de ginepro scorza De cetrangoli foglie de
> saluia foglie De basilico De rosamarino De maiorana fina De menta ro-
> tonda Loribache pulegio gentiana Calamento fior de sambuco rose bian- p. **88**.
>
> 60
> doppia 5)
> 5) D'altro inchiostro nel margine.

Figure 15 Aqua Celeste (Passolini 1893, p639-40)

Piglia garofani, noce moscata, zenzero, pepe lungo, pepe rotondo, grani di ginepro, scorza di cetrangoli, foglie di salvia, di basilico, di rosmarino, di maggiorana fine et di menta, fior di sambuco, rose bianche et rosse [e altri 20 ingredienti, compresi fichi secchi uva passa e miele] Che ogni cosa sia ben polverizzata o pezzi metti in acqua vitae [anche l'acquavite o grappa è spesso consigliata nelle ricette di Caterina]. Metti in una bottiglia ben chiusa et lasciala doi giorni poi metti nel fornello col' alambicco et distilla cinque volte, con fuoco lento, uscirà un'aqua rarissinma e preziosa (Catellani 2014).

Take cloves, nutmeg, mustard, long pepper, round pepper, juniper berries, citron peel, leaves of sage, of basil, of rosemary, of fine marjoram and of mint, elder flowers, white and red roses, [and 20 other ingredients, including dried figs, raisins and honey]. Ensure that everything be well ground up or in pieces [and place] in *acqua vita* [a distilled wine spirit often used in Catherine's recipes]. Place in a well closed bottle and leave it for two days then put in an alembic [still] and distill five times, with a slow fire, there will come out a water most rare and precious.

610 GLI *EXPERIMENTI*

che et roscie spigo nardo Legno aloes Culebe [1]) Domestiche et Saluatiche Cardamomo cinamomo fino calamo romatico Sticados Camadreos Camapiteos Meligetto mastico incenso bianco aloe patico Semenza et foglia Di anesi Semenza de artemisia an grossi. 1. fichi secchi vna passa vltra marina et [2]) Carne de Dattili mandole Dolce pignoli mandole amare an on. 1. mele spumato on VI poi tolli tanto zuccaro fino che sia el doppio de tutte le ditte cose et omne cosa per se sia Bene puluirazata quelle che se possino poluerizare et le altre

p. **89.** siano peste inseme, le quale [3]) le quale [3]) tutte cose ut supra poluerizate et peste incorporate [4]) inseme et mettile in tanta acqua de uita che sia tre uolte tanto a peso quanto sonno le sopra ditte cose la quale acqua sia destillata cinque volte alanbicco de vetro pigliando sempre la Bona et questo fatto metti tutte le ditte cose in lacqua de vita una bozza ben chiusa et Lutata et lassala star cusi per dui di naturale et poi mettilo nel suo fornello col suo Lanbicco Lutato le iunture fa destillare con foco Lento et meglio seria con Bagnio maria et uscira una acqua chiarissima et pretiosa et continua lo lo [5]) foco per fin tanto che lacqua mutera colore et come tu uedi venir

p. **90.**

[1]) *Forse manca il nome di un ingrediente.*

[2]) *Aggiunto nell' interlineo.*

[3])-[3]) *Ripetuto per errore.*

[4]) *L. forse* "incorporale."

[5]) *Ripetuto per errore.*

Figure 16 Aqua Celeste (Passolini 1893, p639-40)

Conclusion

I had so much fun translating Caterina's recipes! I was able to practice my amateur skill of translating and learned a lot in the process. I also learned more about Caterina's life, her worries, her triumphs, and about period alchemy than I knew before. I'm one step closer to being the best Giata Alberti of 1499 I can be, and I have a slew of new recipes to redact and add to my toilette. I don't consider the few dead ends (*zusvese*, *tirats*, *botto*) I ran into to be failures, I look at them as future opportunities. I will keep trying to find the words as they are and also to deduce the root or suffix etymology that may just land me the solution to these mysteries. This is one of the beauties of reenacting and adopting the medieval mindset; the journey counts more than the destination.

Glossary

From Florio (1611) and Barnhart (1995)

Aceto = Vinegar (from Latin acetum "vinegar")
Acqua vita = distilled wine
Alambicco, lanbicco, bagno maria = Alembic (still, from Middle French *alambic* (13c.))
Alume de rocco = Rock alum (from Latin alumen)
Aqua de rosa = Rosewater (Latin rosa)
Argento Vivo = Quicksilver
Bagno maria = Alembic
Basilico = Basil (from Medieval Latin basilicum)
Bottiglia ben chiusa = Well-closed bottle
Botte = ?
Bryonia = Bryonia dioica
Bulbo del giglio = Bulb of lily
Guscio d'uovo = Eggshell (from Latin ovum "egg")
Raschiatura d'avorio = Ivory scrapings (from Latin eboreus "of ivory,")
Calcina viva = Quicklime (A loan-translation of Latin calx viva)
Camomila = Chamomile
Canfora = Camphor
Cannella = Cinnamon
Cedro = Cedar (Latin cedrus, from Greek kedros "cedar, juniper,")
Cenere = Ashes
Cerusica = White lead (from Latin *cerussa)*
Cerussa = White lead (from Latin *cerussa)*
Chiara de ove = Egg white (from Latin ovum "egg")
Cinabro = Cinnabar
Cinamomi = Cinnamon
Crusca di grano finche = Wheat bran
Distilla = Distill (from Latin distillare)
Ellera = Ivy
Edera = Ivy
Farina = Flour
Fichi secchi = Figs dried (from Latin ficus)
Fior di sambuco = Elderflowers
Foglie = Leaves
Foglie di salvia = Leave of sage (Salvia officinalis)
Fuoco = Fire
Galbano = Galbanum, a gum resin from Persia
Garofani = Cloves (from Old French girofle "clove,")
Garofano = Clove
Grani di ginepro = Juniper berries (from Latin juniperus)
Grappa = Acqua vitae (distilled wine)
Gumme edere = Gum ivy (Hedera helix)
Hellera = Ivy

Lanbicco = Alembic (from 13c French alambic, via Old Spanish, from Arabic al-anbiq "distilling flask,")
Libra, Libbra, Livra = Pound (328 grams, Ferrara) made up of 12 onza
Limoni, Limone = Lemons
Lissi = Lye
Maggiorana fine = Marjoram
Malva = Mallow
Masticis = Mastic gum
Menta = Mint (from Latin menta)
Miele crudo= Honey (raw)
Mira el sole = Sunflower (precursor to 1580s Italian girasole, literally "turning toward the sun)
Mirre = Myrrh
Noce moscata, moscati = Nutmeg
Nucis moscate = Nutmeg
Olio, Oleo, Olium = Oil (from Latin oleum)
Oncia, Onza = Ounce (27.25 grams, Ferrara)
Oro = Gold
Orpimento = Orpiment, arsenic trisulphide (from Latin auripigmentum, from aurum "gold" + pigmentum "coloring, pigment, paint)
Ortica = Nettles
Ortica/ Ortiga = Nettle
Ottavi = Eighth (0.0543 liters, Rimini for oil)
Pepe lungo = Long pepper
Pepe rotundo = Round pepper
Pomo = Apple
Prezzemolo = Parsley
Quarta, Quarto = Quarter (0.089 liters for wine, Ferrara,)
Radice = Root
Rosarum = Rose
Rose bianche = White roses (Latin rosa)
Rose rosse = Red roses (Latin rosa)
Rosmarino = Rosemary (from Latin rosmarinus)
Sale = Salt
Salvia = Sage (Salvia officinalis)
Scodella, Scudella = bowl/cup (237 grams, Ferrara)
Scorza = Peel, Score (to cut with incisions or notches," c.1400)
Scorza di cetrangoli = Citron peel
Scrupolo = Scruple (1.0198 grams, Ferrara)
Semenza = Seed (from Latin semen "seed of plants, animals, or men)
Solfo = Sulfur
Storacis calamite = Styrax resin, storax calamite
Tagliato = cut very small
Trifoglio = Clover
Urtica = Nettle (Latin for "nettle, stinging nettle)
Uva passa = Raisin

Violarum = Violet
Violato = Violet (diminutive of viole "violet," from Latin viola "the violet, a violet color,")
Zaffrano = Saffron
Zenzebero = Mustard
Zucchero = Sugar
Zusvese = ?

Bibliography

Barnhart, Robert. (1995). Barnhart Concise Dictionary of Etymology.

Caruso, Elio. (2009). Ricette d'amore e di bellezza di Caterina Sforza: Signora di Forlì e di Imola. Cesena: Ponte Vecchio.

Catellani, Patrizia. (2014). Excerpted Recipes from Gli Experimenti. Retrieved from the University of Pavia Website on 19 May 2014 at http://chifar.unipv.it/museo/Catellani/catSforza/Ric_CatSf.htm

Eamon, William. (1994). Science and the Secrets of Nature: Books of Secrets in Medieval and Early Modern Culture. NJ: Princeton University Press. pp 27, 30, 37, 145-7,164.

Florio, Giovanni. (1611). A Worlde of Wordes: English-Italian Dictionary.

Guerrini, Olindo. (1883). Ricettario galante del principio del secolo xvi. Bologna; Romanoli.

Lev, Elizabeth. (2011). The Tigress of Forli. New York: Mariner

Marriott, John, Keith Wilson, Christopher Langley and Dawn Belcher. (2006). Pharmaceutical Compounding and Dispensing. UK: Pharmaceutical Press. p 38.

Passolini, Pier Desiderio. (1893). Caterina Sforza Volumes I and II. Roma: Loescher.

Passolini, Pier Desiderio. (1893). Caterina Sforza Volume III: Documenti. Roma: Loescher. Retrieved on 4 June 2014 at http://books.google.com/books?id=Aj9WAAAAYAAJ&printsec=frontcover#v=onepage&q&f=false

Rovesti, Paolo. (1975). Alla ricerca dei cosmetici perduti. Venezia: Marsilio.

Salvadori, Roberto. (2003). Il dolore e la sua storia. Regione Toscana.

Scully, Terence (1995). The Art of Cookery in the Middle Ages. Woodbridge UK: Boyhill Press. p 159.

Wheeler, Jo. (2009). Renaissance Secrets: Recipes and Formulas. UK: Victoria & Albert Museum. pp 11, 19, 29, 62.

Zupko, Ronald. (1981). Italian Weights and Measures from the Middle Ages to the Nineteenth Century v145. Philadelphia: American Philosophical Society. http://books.google.com/books?id=GrVoh1JxRRAC&q=onza#v=snippet&q=1&f=false

APPENDICES

Appendix A – Gli Experimenti Recipes (from Passolini 1893)

Appendix A – Gli Experimenti Recipes (from Passolini Volume III, 1893)

All images of recipes throughout this booklet originate from this open source document printed in 1893.

Made in United States
Orlando, FL
21 May 2022